SIMPLE MACHINE PROJECTS

Making Machines with Levers

Chris Oxlade

heinemann
raintree

© 2015 Heinemann Raintree
an imprint of Capstone Global Library, LLC
Chicago, Illinois

To contact Capstone Global Library, please call 800-747-4992,
or visit our web site www.capstonepub.com

Edited by James Benefield and Erika Shores
Designed by Steve Mead
Original illustrations © Capstone Global Library Ltd 2015
Picture research by Jo Miller
Production by Victoria Fitzgerald
Originated by Capstone Global Library Ltd
Printed and bound in China by Leo Paper Group

18 17 16 15 14
10 9 8 7 6 5 4 3 2 1

Library of Congress Cataloging-in-Publication Data
Oxlade, Chris, author.
  Making machines with levers / Chris Oxlade.
     pages cm.—(Simple machine projects)

  ISBN 978-1-4109-6799-2 (hb)—ISBN 978-1-4109-6806-7
(pb)—ISBN 978-1-4109-6820-3 (ebook) 1. Levers—Juvenile
literature. 2. Simple machines—Juvenile literature. I. Title.

TJ147.O86 2015
  621.8'11—dc23   2014013705

**This book has been officially leveled by using the F&P Text
Level Gradient™ Leveling System.**

Acknowledgments
We would like to thank the following for permission to repro-
duce photographs:

All photos Capstone Studio: Karon Dubke except: Alamy: Caro,
18; Dreamstime: Puma330, 4, Vitaly Titov & Maria Sidelniko-
va, 29 (bottom); Photoshot/Eye Ubiquitous, 12; Shutterstock:
Alenavlad, 25, c12, 27, John Kropewnicki, 19, roger pilkington,
29 (top), Vadim Ratnikov, 26; SSPL via Getty Images, 13; Wiki-
media: Sébastien Savard, 24.

Design Elements: Shutterstock: Timo Kohlbacher.

We would like to thank Harold Pratt and Richard Taylor for
their invaluable help in the preparation of this book.

Every effort has been made to contact copyright holders
of material reproduced in this book. Any omissions will
be rectified in subsequent printings if notice is given to
the publisher.

All the Internet addresses (URLs) given in this book were valid
at the time of going to press. However, due to the dynamic
nature of the Internet, some addresses may have changed, or
sites may have changed or ceased to exist since publication.
While the author and publisher regret any inconvenience this
may cause readers, no responsibility for any such changes can
be accepted by either the author or the publisher.

CONTENTS

Some words are shown in bold, **like this**. You can find out what they mean by looking in the glossary.

WHAT IS A LEVER?

Have you ever cut paper with scissors or broken open a nut with a nutcracker? Then levers have helped you!

A lever is a simple machine. Simple machines make our lives easier by helping us to do jobs such as lifting heavy loads, gripping objects, and cutting materials. In this book, you'll see many examples of levers, and the activities will help you to understand how levers work.

Have you ever played on something like this? Can you see the levers in action?

Levers everywhere

Scissors and nutcrackers are just some of the household tools and gadgets that rely on levers to work. Other levers you might find in your house might include can openers, bottle openers, some faucet handles, hammers, and pliers.

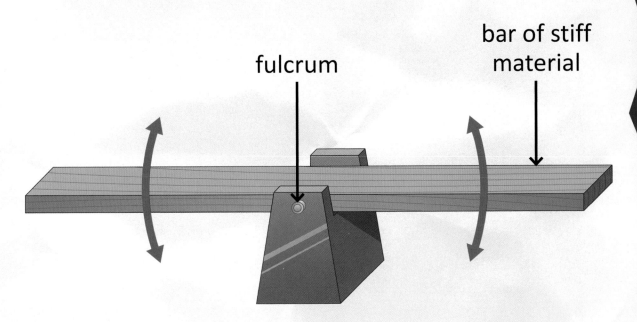

fulcrum

bar of stiff material

 A lever is made up of a bar, fixed at a **fulcrum** (pivot).

HOW LEVERS WORK

When you push (or pull) on one part of a lever, the lever pushes (or pulls) on the object you want to move, squeeze, or cut. A seesaw is a lever. One child's weight (how heavy he or she is) lifts another child's weight.

One lever or two?

Some tools, such as a bottle opener and a crowbar, are made up of a single lever. But many tools and gadgets, such as scissors and pliers, are made up of two levers joined together.

FORCE AND MOTION

Simple machines such as levers can change force and **motion**. A simple machine can make a force (a push or a pull) larger or smaller, or change the direction of a force. It can also make a movement larger or smaller, or change the direction of a movement.

Three types of levers

There are three different types of lever. In each type, the fulcrum (the place where you pull or push) and the position of the object being moved or cut is different. The project on the next page will help you to understand what each type of lever does.

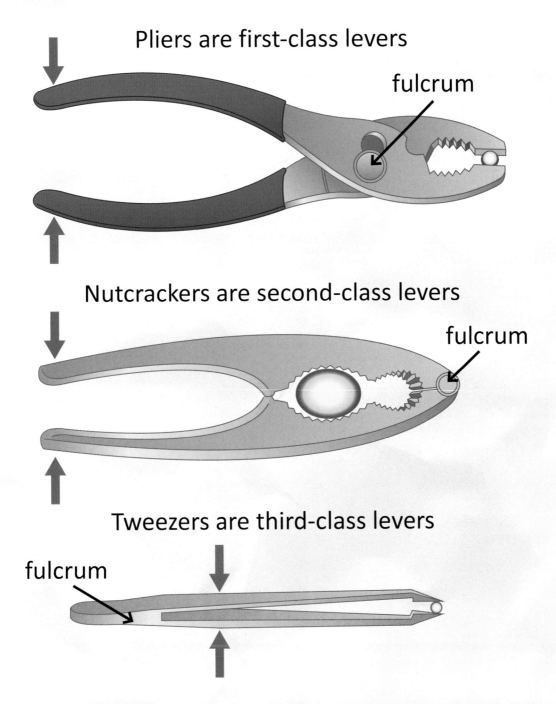

Pliers are first-class levers

fulcrum

Nutcrackers are second-class levers

fulcrum

Tweezers are third-class levers

fulcrum

Different Levers

Here's how to make tools that use the three different types of lever (see page 7). You can test how each type of lever changes forces and motion.

What you need:
- a pen
- small rubber bands
- 2 wooden or stiff plastic 12-in. (30-cm) rulers
- a thick pen (such as a marker pen)

A first-class lever

1 Place the pen on a table and rest the center of the ruler on the pen. Use a rubber band to join the ruler and pen together, as shown.

STEP 1

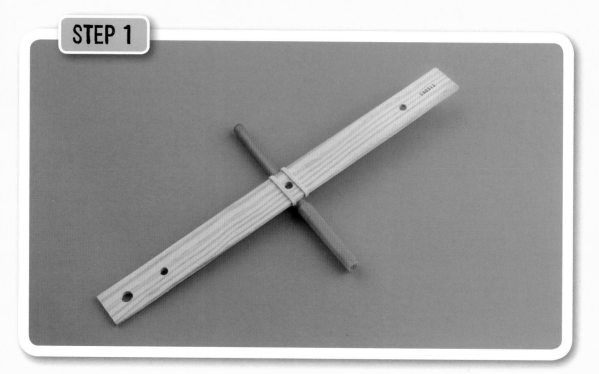

2 Put one finger from each hand on each end of the ruler. Can you feel that when you push down with one finger, you push up the other finger?

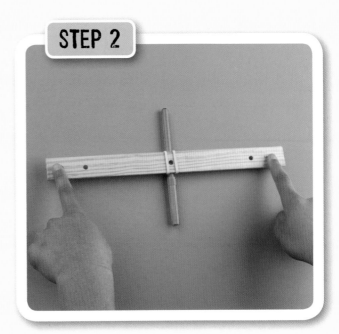

Bigger forces

3 Now slide the pen along until it is about 2 in. (5 cm) from one end of the ruler. Put your fingers on the ends of the ruler again. Can you feel that a small downward push on the long end makes a larger upward push at the short end?

STEP 3

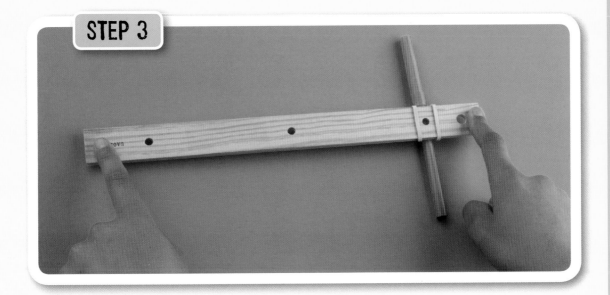

A second-class lever

4 Take the pen off the ruler. Get the second ruler and put the two rulers face to face, with the pen in between them, about 1 in. (2 cm) from one end.

5 Put a rubber band around the long ends of the rulers. Slide the rubber band along until it is next to the pen. Twist the rubber band and loop it over the short ends of the rulers.

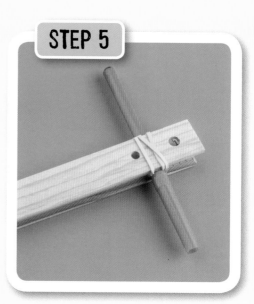

STEP 5

6 Put a finger in between the rulers, close to the pencil. Squeeze the two ends together with the other hand. Do the levers change how much you push?

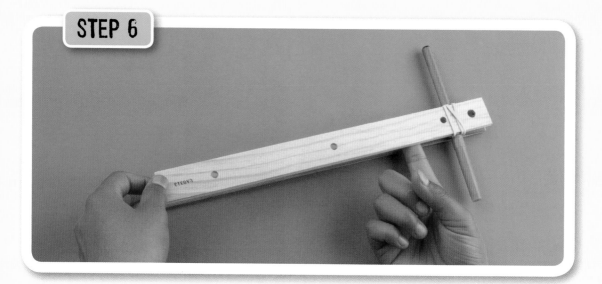

STEP 6

A third-class lever

7 Now put a finger between the ends of the rulers, and hold the rulers close to the pen with the other hand. What do the levers do to your push this time?

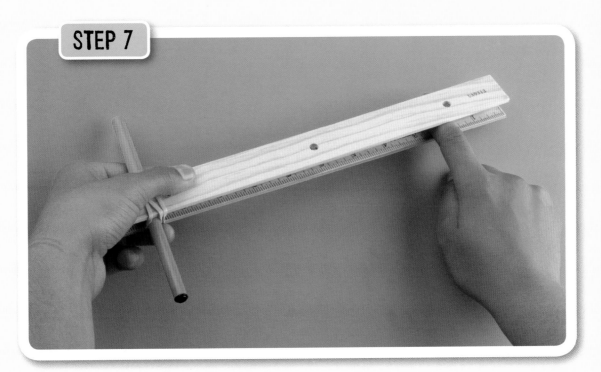

STEP 7

What did you find out?

This project shows that levers can be arranged in different ways to make forces bigger and smaller. First-class levers can make forces bigger or smaller, second-class levers always make forces bigger, and third-class levers always make forces smaller.

LEVERS IN HISTORY

The lever is not a new idea! People understood levers thousands of years ago. They put them to work to do the same jobs they do today—to lift and move heavy things, and to squeeze and cut materials.

Lifting water

A shaduf is an ancient machine used to raise water. The weight of a big rock, and a pull from a farmer, on one end of a wooden lever lifts a heavy bucket of water on the other end of the lever. In some places, farmers still use this simple tool today.

The heavy stone on this shaduf is helping the farmer to lift a bucket of water.

Weighing goods

Roman tradesmen weighed their goods with levers. A Roman **weighing machine** was made up of a metal bar suspended near the center. A weight was moved along the bar to make the bar balance.

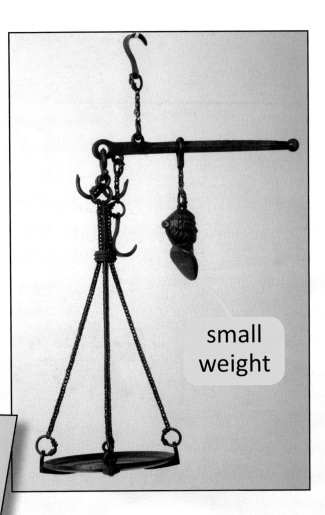

small weight

The position of the weight showed the size of the weight in the pan.

MOVING THE EARTH

The mathematician Archimedes, from ancient Greece, realized how powerful levers could be. He said that if he had a lever long enough and he had a place to put the fulcrum, he could move Earth with his hands.

Make Some Scales

This project will show how a Roman weighing machine, or scale, worked.

1 Cut out a thin rectangle from one side of the piece of cardboard, as shown in the picture. You can use a ruler.

What you need:
- a 12-in. (30-cm) plastic ruler
- a pencil
- thin, letter-sized cardboard
- a medium-sized rubber band
- two small toy wooden blocks
- a small plastic bottle cap (about 1½ in., or 4 cm, across)
- five same-sized washers
- sticky tape
- all-purpose glue

STEP 1

2 Put the cardboard rectangle on top of the ruler. Tape it in place at the ends and at the middle.

STEP 2

3 Place the pencil on top of the ruler, in the center of the ruler (see picture for step five).

4 Wrap a rubber band around the ruler and the pencil. This will keep the pencil and the ruler together (again, see the picture for step five).

5 Glue the plastic lid, upside down, onto the cardboard, 2 in. (5 cm) from the pencil.

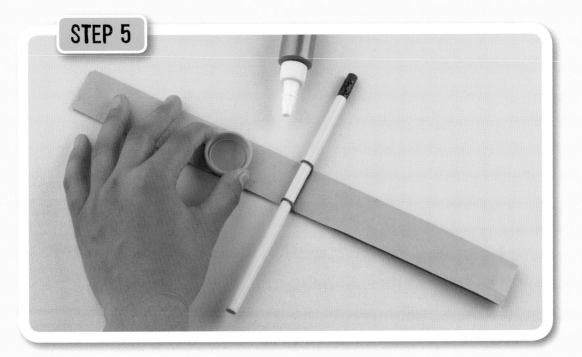

STEP 5

6 Rest the pencil on the two wooden blocks, as shown in the picture for step 7. Move the pencil along the ruler until the ruler balances.

7 Put one washer in the lid. Put another washer on the other end of the ruler. Move this washer back and forth until the ruler balances.

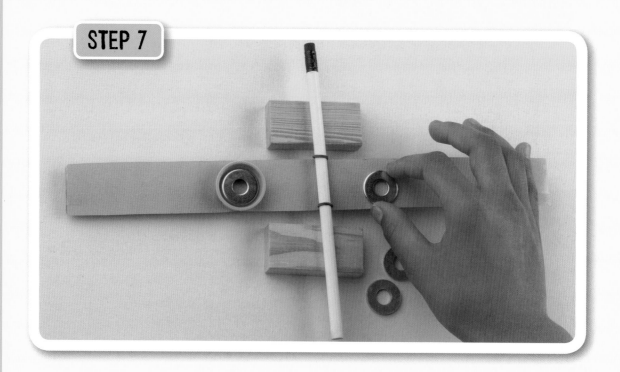

STEP 7

8 Draw a line level with the center of the washer and write "1" next to the line.

9 Add another washer to the lid. Move the single washer to balance the ruler again. Make another mark and write "2" next to it.

10 Repeat step 9, using three and then four washers in the lid. Now you have a scale on the ruler.

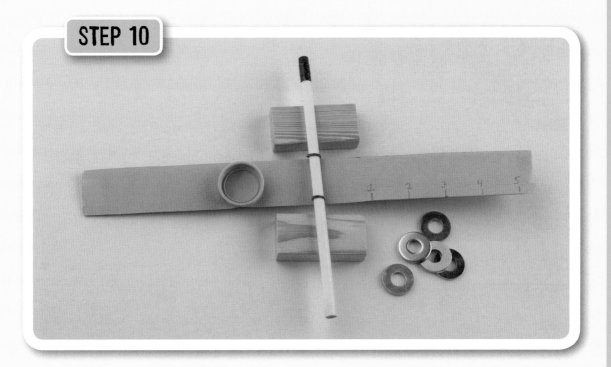

STEP 10

11 Put a small object in the lid Move the single washer to balance the ruler. How many washers does your object weigh?

What did you find out?

The ruler works like a weighing machine. It shows how many washers an object weighs. The farther along the ruler you have to move the single washer, the heavier the object in the tray is.

CHANGING FORCES AND MOTION

When you push or pull on one part of a lever, the lever makes a larger or smaller push on another object. But the farther away from the fulcrum you push or pull, the bigger effect your push or pull has.

A lug **wrench** is a tool for tightening the lug nuts on a car wheel. It has a very long handle, so a good push at the end of the wrench tightens the nut very securely.

This lug wrench has two long levers, so the driver can tighten the lug nuts.

An oar is a long lever. The fulcrum is the oar holder on the side of the boat.

Levers can also change motion, making a movement much greater. If you move one part of a lever a small distance, another part moves a much greater distance. Rowing is a good example. A rower pulls the handle of an oar a short distance, and the blade of the oar (in the picture above, the orange end of the oar) moves much farther through the water.

GIANT WRENCHES

The parts of a building's **steel frame** are joined together with huge nuts and bolts. Workers tighten the nuts and bolts with very long wrenches.

Magnifying Motion

This project shows how levers can change motion, turning a small movement into a large movement.

What you need:
- a piece of stiff cardboard (letter size)
- some more stiff cardboard
- a ruler
- a pen
- paper fasteners
- a sharp pencil

1 Cut two strips of cardboard 8 x 1 in. (20 x 3 cm) and one strip 6 x 1 in. (15 x 3 cm).

2 In one 8-x-1-inch strip, pierce a hole 2 in. (5 cm) from one end. Don't push the pencil through. On the cardboard, write "A" by the hole. Then, pierce a small hole half an inch (1½ cm) from the other end. Write "B" next to it.

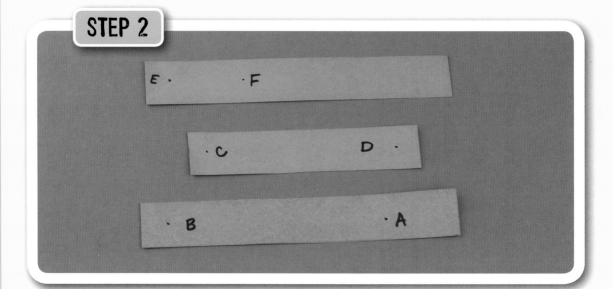

STEP 2

3 In the second 8-x-1-inch strip, pierce a hole half an inch from one end. Write "E" next to it. Then, make a second hole, hole "F," 2 inches from Hole E.

4 In the last strip, pierce a hole half an inch from each end. Label the holes "C" and "D" (see step 2 picture).

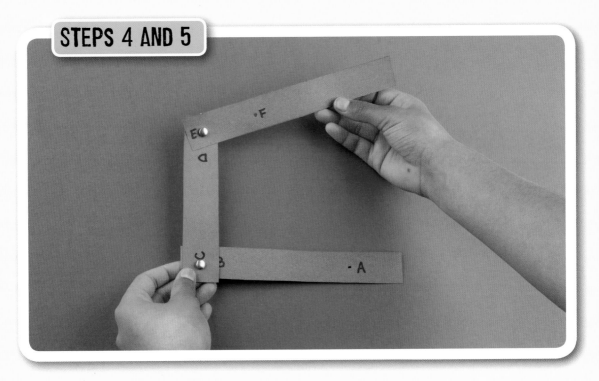

STEPS 4 AND 5

5 Connect holes B to C, and holes D to E, with the paper fasteners.

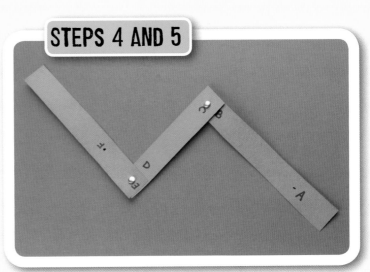

STEPS 4 AND 5

6 Get the cardboard. Pierce a small hole 1½ in. (4 cm) from one long edge (see picture). Pierce a hole 1½ inches inside from one corner on the other edge.

STEP 6

7 Connect the strips to the cardboard with paper fasteners, through these holes. Experiment with fasteners to see where you need to place them.

STEP 7

8 Put your hand on a sheet of cardboard and draw around it. Cut out the hand and tape it to the long cardboard arm (see picture at right).

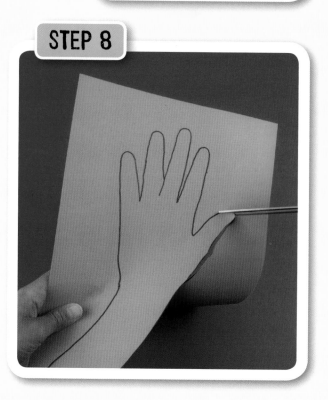

STEP 8

9 Move the lever arm (as shown, below) from side to side to make the hand wave!

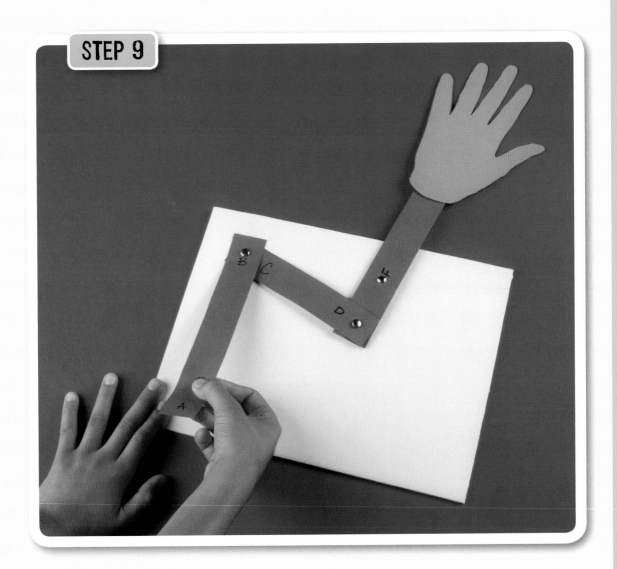

STEP 9

What did you find out?
Working together, the two levers make a small movement of your fingers into a much larger movement of the waving hand.

EVERYDAY LEVERS

We use levers in all sorts of places. Some, such as scissors, are easy to see, but others are not so obvious.

Cantilever bridges

Many bridges rely on levers to stay up. One sort of bridge that relies on the lever is the cantilever bridge. The bridge itself is a lever. One end of the lever stretches out over the water, and the other end is connected to the ground.

This is a cantilever bridge being built. Each side is a lever.

Some musical instruments rely on levers, too. All the keys on a piano keyboard are levers. So are the foot pedals. When you press a key down, the other end of the key pushes up. It presses on another lever called the hammer, and the hammer hits a string to play a note.

When a piano player presses on a key, levers make a hammer swing and hit a string to play a note.

LEVERS IN YOUR BODY

You even have levers in your body. Your lower arm is a lever. Your elbow is its fulcrum, and it is moved up and down by your bicep muscle in your upper arm.

LEVERS IN COMPLEX MACHINES

Many complicated machines contain simple machines such as levers. Construction machines such as backhoes and cranes use levers to lift and move materials. The arm of a backhoe is made up of levers. In the driver's cab, there are levers that the driver uses to control the backhoe, to move the arm and digging bucket.

Hydraulic rams push and pull on one end of the levers in this backhoe's arm.

Bicycles also have levers. You pull brake levers on the handlebars, which pull cables attached to the brakes. At the brakes, the cables move levers that press rubber brake blocks onto the wheels to slow them.

Take a look at your own bicycle to see the levers that work the brakes.

THE LONGEST LEVERS

Booms are long arms of cranes. They act as super-long levers. A huge concrete weight on one end of the boom holds up the other end of the boom and the load hanging from it.

FACTS AND FUN

AMAZING LEVERS

The longest cantilever bridge in the world is the Pont de Quebec, in Quebec, Canada. It is 1,801 feet (549 meters) long.

There are even levers in space! The robot arm on the International Space Station is made up of thin levers and is 56 feet (17 meters) long.

Humans are not the only creatures to use levers. Orangutans use sticks as levers to open tasty fruits.

The longest seesaw in the world was built by Ashrita Furman of New York. It is 79 feet (24 meters) long.

The Kroll K-10000 tower crane has an arm 330 feet (100 meters) long. It's the longest arm of any tower crane.

LEVERS TODAY

All simple machines, including levers, were invented thousands of years ago. The lever may have been invented around 200,000 years ago. It's amazing that levers are just as important today as they were then. We often use levers in complex modern machines, but also for the same jobs that people used them for all that time ago. And the lever will probably be useful for many years to come!

Where and what are these levers?

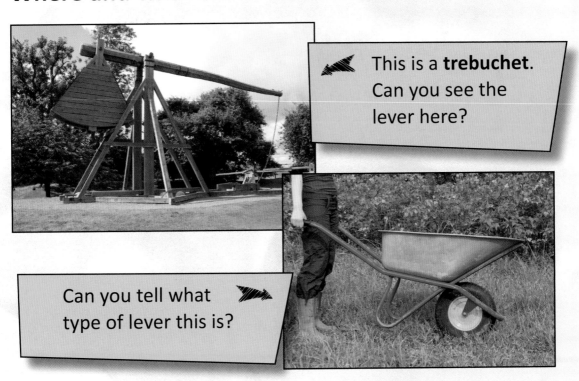

This is a **trebuchet**. Can you see the lever here?

Can you tell what type of lever this is?

GLOSSARY

fulcrum point around which a lever rotates

hydraulic ram piston pushed out of a cylinder by liquid, used to move parts of large machines such as backhoes

motion another way of saying movement

pulley simple machine made up of wheels and rope, used to lift or pull objects

ramp simple machine used to lift heavy objects

screw simple machine that has a spiral-shaped thread, used to attach or lift materials

spring device that can be pressed or pulled but that returns to its first shape when released

steel frame steel skeleton that holds up a building

trebuchet medieval weapon. It works like a catapult.

wedge simple machine used to split apart materials

weighing machine machine that measures the force that pulls an object toward the ground

wheel and axle simple machine made up of a wheel on an axle, used to turn or lift objects

wrench tool for tightening or loosening a nut or bolt

FIND OUT MORE

Books

Deane-Pratt, Ade. *Simple Machines* (How Things Work). New York: PowerKids, 2012.

Oxlade, Chris. *Levers* (Simple Machines). North Mankato, Minn.: Smart Apple Media, 2008.

Walker, Sally M., and Roseann Feldmann. *Put Levers to the Test* (How Do Simples Machines Work?). Minneapolis: Lerner, 2012.

Web sites

Facthound offers a safe, fun way to find Internet sites related to this book. All of the sites on Facthound have been researched by our staff.

Here's all you do:
Visit *www.facthound.com*
Type in this code: 9781410967992

INDEX